Date: 7/9/21

BR 613.4 MIN
Minden, Cecilia.
Keep it clean. Time to wash
up /

21st Century Basic Skills Library

KEEP IT CLEAN TIME TO WASH UP

by Cecilia Minden, PhD

Cherry Lake Publishing • Ann Arbor, Michigan

1

CHERRY LAKE
Publishing

Published in the United States of America
by Cherry Lake Publishing
Ann Arbor, Michigan
www.cherrylakepublishing.com

Photo Credits: Cover and page 1, ©iStockphoto.com/michellegibson;
page 4, ©iStockphoto.com/ND1939; page 6, ©iStockphoto.com/
Henrik5000; page 8, ©Larisa Lofitskaya/Shutterstock, Inc.; page 10,
©iStockphoto.com/jorgeantonio; page 12, ©picturepartners/Shutterstock,
Inc.; page 14, ©iStockphoto.com/squadcsplayer; page 16, ©Leah-Anne
Thompson/Shutterstock, Inc.; page 18, ©Baileyone/Shutterstock, Inc.;
page 20, ©Monkey Business Images/Shutterstock, Inc.

Library of Congress Cataloging-in-Publication Data
Minden, Cecilia.
  Keep it clean: time to wash up/by Cecilia Minden.
    p. cm.—(21st century basic skills library level 1)
  Includes bibliographical references and index.
  ISBN-13: 978-1-60279-855-7 (lib. bdg.)
  ISBN-10: 1-60279-855-9 (lib. bdg.)
  1. Hand washing—Juvenile literature. I. Title.
  RA777.M56 2010
  613'.4—dc22   2009048572

Cherry Lake Publishing would like to acknowledge
the work of The Partnership for 21st Century Skills.
Please visit *www.21stcenturyskills.org* for more information.

Printed in the United States of America
Corporate Graphics Inc.
August 2011
CLFA07

TABLE OF CONTENTS

5 A Handful of Germs

11 How to Wash

17 When to Wash

22 Find Out More

22 Glossary

23 Home and School Connection

24 Index

24 About the Author

A Handful of Germs

Your hands get dirty every day.

Germs are in the dirt.

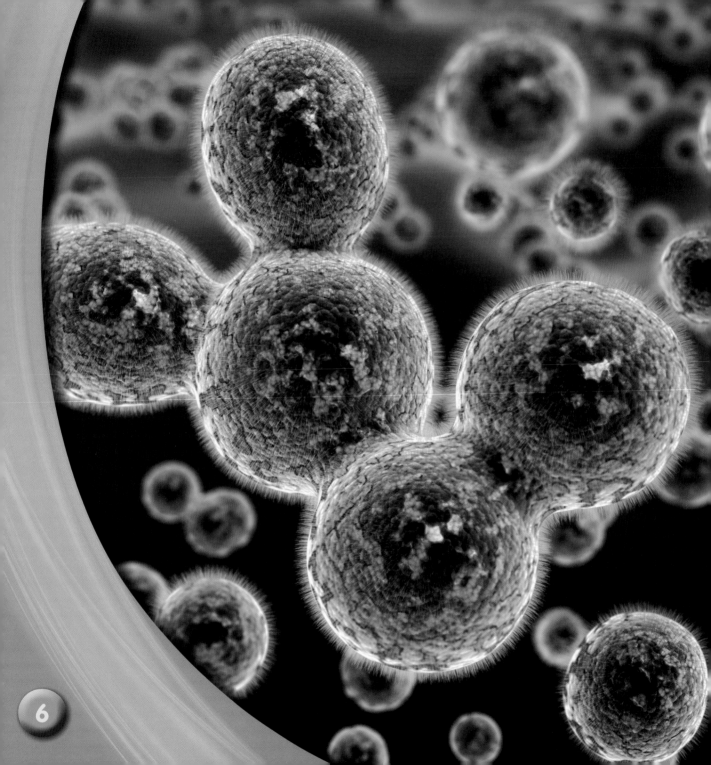

You cannot see germs.

Some germs can make us sick.

Germs get on our hands.

That is why we wash our hands.

How to Wash

Lather with soap and water.

Put them all over your hands.

Sing a song while you wash.

Make those germs go away!

Now **rinse** your hands.

Dry them with a clean **towel**.

When to Wash

Wash after you play with toys.

Wash after you use the bathroom.

Wash after you play with pets.

Wash after you play outside.

Always wash before you eat.

When will you wash?

Find Out More

BOOK

Royston, Angela. *Why Do I Wash My Hands*? Mankato, MN: QEB
 Publishing, 2010.

WEB SITE

NSF Scrub Club
www.scrubclub.org/site/meet.aspx
Meet the Scrub Club and learn more about the proper way to
wash your hands.

Glossary

germs (JERMZ) tiny living things we cannot see that spread
illnesses

lather (LATH-ur) to create foam by rubbing soap and water on skin

rinse (RINSS) to run clean water over something to remove soap
or dirt

towel (TOU-uhl) a cloth used for drying or wiping

Home and School Connection

Use this list of words from the book to help your child become a better reader. Word games and writing activities can help beginning readers reinforce literacy skills.

a	eat	outside	to
after	every	over	towel
all	germs	pets	toys
always	get	play	us
and	go	put	use
are	handful	rinse	wash
away	hands	see	water
bathroom	how	sick	we
before	in	sing	when
can	is	soap	while
cannot	lather	song	why
clean	make	some	will
day	now	that	with
dirt	of	the	you
dirty	on	them	your
dry	our	those	

Index

bathroom, 17

drying, 15

eating, 21

germs, 5, 7, 9, 13

hands, 5, 9, 11, 15

lather, 11

pets, 19
playing, 17, 19

rinsing, 15

sickness, 7
singing, 13

soap, 11

towels, 15

washing, 9, 11, 13, 17, 19, 21
water, 11

About the Author

Cecilia Minden is the former Director of the Language and Literacy Program at the Harvard Graduate School of Education. She currently works as a literacy consultant for school and library publishers and is the author of more than 100 books for children.